YOU WILL BE A GREAT COOK

You Will Be A Great Cook

Read Daily for Affirmation Book Series

Walter the Educator

SILENT KING BOOKS

SKB

Copyright © 2024 by Walter the Educator

All rights reserved. No part of this book may be reproduced in any manner whatsoever without written permission except in the case of brief quotations embodied in critical articles and reviews.

First Printing, 2024

Disclaimer
This book is a literary work; poems are not about specific persons, locations, situations, and/or circumstances unless mentioned in a historical context. This book is for entertainment and informational purposes only. The author and publisher offer this information without warranties expressed or implied. No matter the grounds, neither the author nor the publisher will be accountable for any losses, injuries, or other damages caused by the reader's use of this book. The use of this book acknowledges an understanding and acceptance of this disclaimer.

dedicated to those that want to be a great cook

YOU WILL BE A GREAT COOK

I find in soup, a comfort true,

You Will Be A Great Cook

In every broth, a strength anew,

You Will Be A Great Cook

Stews that bubble, rich and hearty,

You Will Be A Great Cook

In this feast, I'm a part of the party.

You Will Be A Great Cook

Salads crisp, like morning dew,

You Will Be A Great Cook

Colors bright, a vibrant hue,

You Will Be A Great Cook

Vinaigrettes with tangy flair,

You Will Be A Great Cook

In each bite, a love affair.

You Will Be A Great Cook

The grill, a fiery dragon's lair,

You Will Be A Great Cook

Yet I, unflinching, dare to care,

You Will Be A Great Cook

Char and smoke, a flavor bold,

You Will Be A Great Cook

In this heat, my skills unfold.

You Will Be A Great Cook

Seasoning with a careful hand,

You Will Be A Great Cook

Salt and pepper, grains of sand,

You Will Be A Great Cook

Balancing flavors, just so right,

You Will Be A Great Cook

In every dish, a dance of light.

You Will Be A Great Cook

I plate with care, a work of art,

You Will Be A Great Cook

Each element, a beating heart,

You Will Be A Great Cook

Garnish with a tender touch,

You Will Be A Great Cook

Beauty in simplicity, not too much.

You Will Be A Great Cook

I am the alchemist, turning base,

You Will Be A Great Cook

To golden dishes, filled with grace,

You Will Be A Great Cook

In every course, a testament,

You Will Be A Great Cook

To love, to life, a grand ascent.

You Will Be A Great Cook

In every kitchen's sacred space,

You Will Be A Great Cook

I find my rhythm, set my pace,

You Will Be A Great Cook

Creating joy, one meal at a time,

You Will Be A Great Cook

In this craft, I find my prime.

You Will Be A Great Cook

So, I declare with passion's fire,

You Will Be A Great Cook

"I will be a great cook," my desire,

You Will Be A Great Cook

With every meal, a journey grand,

You Will Be A Great Cook

In my heart, I firmly stand.

You Will Be A Great Cook

For in each dish, a part of me,

You Will Be A Great Cook

In every bite, a legacy,

You Will Be A Great Cook

Through taste and texture, sight and smell,

You Will Be A Great Cook

I weave my dreams, I cast my spell.

You Will Be A Great Cook

So here I stand, with pride unshook,

You Will Be A Great Cook

"I will be a great cook," in every book,

You Will Be A Great Cook

With every dish, I write my name,

You Will Be A Great Cook

In the culinary hall of fame.

You Will Be A Great Cook

ABOUT THE CREATOR

Walter the Educator is one of the pseudonyms for Walter Anderson. Formally educated in Chemistry, Business, and Education, he is an educator, an author, a diverse entrepreneur, and he is the son of a disabled war veteran. "Walter the Educator" shares his time between educating and creating. He holds interests and owns several creative projects that entertain, enlighten, enhance, and educate, hoping to inspire and motivate you.

> Follow, find new works, and stay up to date
> with Walter the Educator™
> at WaltertheEducator.com

www.ingramcontent.com/pod-product-compliance
Lightning Source LLC
LaVergne TN
LVHW051921060526
838201LV00060B/4114